Make Money Online Entrepreneur Series:

Book 1

Freeing Up Your Time – VA's, Outsourcing & Goal Setting

KIP PIPER
http://www.kippiperbooks.com

YOUR FREE GIFT...

Want a free book? Want access to more freebies and special offers through Amazon?

As a way of saying *thanks* for your purchase, I'm offering a free eBook that is only available to my customers. Right now, you can get a copy of my book: *"28-Day Small Business Profit Plan: The Quick Start Guide for Business Success"*. This book is not sold anywhere else and can only be found on my website.

Plus, you will learn how to get instant notification whenever there is a **new free book** or **special book bundles** through Amazon.

Get the details at my website: **www.KipPiperBooks.com**

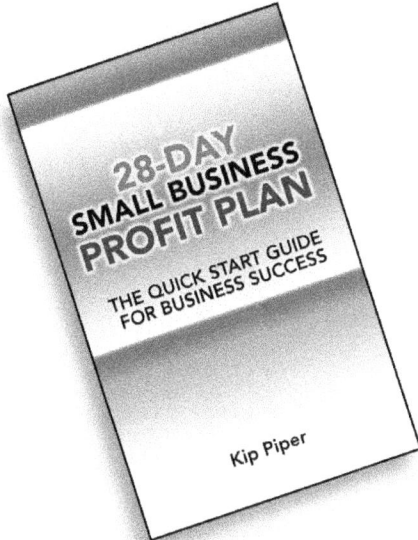

CONTENTS

AUTHOR'S NOTE

As you have probably experienced, the Internet and the websites on it are constantly changing. The information, examples, and screenshots presented in this book are accurate at the time of publication.

If you encounter any websites that have changed, please let me know by emailing me at: kip@kippiperbooks.com.

Remember, even though the website(s) may have changed, the principles, techniques and strategies in this book remain sound.

For your convenience, all websites, tools, and software mentioned in this book are listed in the RESOURCES section at the end of this book.

The links provided are primarily affiliate links, which means if you purchase through the links, the price is the same to you and I receive a commission. This is the heart of affiliate marketing and entrepreneurship – which I am teaching you how to do with this book! I thank you in advance for using the affiliate links.

A FEW WORDS FROM KIP

Before I began teaching others how to blog and be successful with their online businesses, I wanted to be sure that I had something different to teach – strategies that are not easily found but can make a huge impact on success. The last thing I wanted to do is waste anyone's time. I wanted to offer something unique that would add both value and the potential for quick success for you.

Unknowingly, my research into online business success began in 1996 when I was first introduced to the concept of affiliate marketing. The potential for income excited me and I was quick to start experimenting with it. I joined Amazon.com and the few other affiliate programs available at the time. I added links on my website to products that related to my web design and Internet marketing business, with the purpose of offering quality resources to my website visitors and my clients. I encouraged and worked with my clients to include affiliate marketing in their overall online presence. I did this all in the hopes of adding to my income streams and eventually have affiliate marketing my dominant, if not sole, source of income.

But it did not come quickly, as others had promised or experienced. I totally, 100% believed in the concept of an online business and affiliate marketing (and still do), I understood the mechanics of setting up websites, creating products, and adding affiliate links, but I struggled with ranking my site high with the search engines and driving traffic to my site. Where were all the promised visitors who would buy what I offered or recommended so I could earn commissions?

Why were so many others achieving success? Why wasn't I experiencing the same success? Where was I going wrong?

I joined various mastermind groups. I purchased training programs from so-called "gurus". I bought books, read articles, watched videos, attended conference calls and webinars – I immersed myself in learning about blogging, affiliate marketing, and creating products.

The one most important thing I learned is that you need multiple websites, each focused on a different niche, to ensure a steady stream of income. "But," I asked, "if I can't get people to come to my first website, why should I spend more money and time creating websites that will not be visited either?" And each "guru" smiled nicely and said, "If you will upgrade your membership to our most expensive level, I'll tell you." But when I looked closely, I realized each "guru" was not living the life I wanted. In fact, most were working as hard or harder than I – with even less free time and income! They did not have the freedom of time and money that I wanted.

I didn't give up, though. I continued my search – knowing the one little "missing link" was out there.

One day I found it!

With this new knowledge, I knew without a doubt I could not only be personally successful with blogging, affiliate marketing and product creation, but now I could teach others those same strategies.

I realized that knowledge is what sets apart the training I offer – with this book and my other books which you can find at **http://www.kippiperbooks.com**.

This book is unique because it was written for *YOU*.

- YOU are someone who sees the potential in having an online business of affiliate marketing and product creation, but needs to know how to get started.
- YOU want practical strategies and advice that have already been tested and proven to work.
- YOU are ready for double-digit growth in sales.
- YOU are committed to following through with what you're about to learn.

This is why YOU are here.

Now please understand. Every piece of advice, strategy and practice has been tested on actual live blog, affiliate marketing and product websites – my own, my clients', and others. None of this is theory. You might then ask yourself, *ok, so how many blogs and affiliate websites has Kip done and what qualifies her as an "internet business expert"?* I think that's a great question. I wish more people questioned so called "experts" to see what qualifies them. As for me, I looked back on the last 15 years of stats and discovered that I have personally generated a 5-figure income in blogging, affiliate marketing and my own product sales – and that's just part-time!

If that's something you'd like to accomplish, you've selected the right book and series to begin with. I say "begin" because you'll soon discover that the learning process is a journey.

But don't worry! There's one more thing that qualifies me to lead you down this path – I'm just like you. It doesn't matter if you've never built a website or if you're already earning an income with blogging, affiliate marketing and your own product, and simply want to improve your sales. As you have already read, I've been wherever you are right now.

For anyone who reads this book and the entire *"Make Money Online Entrepreneur Series"*, and implements everything they learn, I can guarantee your business will move forward with more subscribers, sales and a stronger connection to your market. Like I said before, it doesn't matter if you've never built a website in your life or if you're already experienced, I've been there and can show you how to make blogging, affiliate marketing and product creation a successful income source.

But before we begin, I need you to do something. Connect with me on Facebook at:

http://www.facebook.com/TheRandomBlondeFanPage

I'd love to stay in touch and learn more about your journey.

You also are invited to check my website for more business books, and all of the books included in this *"Making Money Online Entrepreneur Series"*:

http://www.kippiperbooks.com

Thanks again for choosing to spend this time with me. Now let's get started!

"Done is better than Perfect!"

INTRODUCTION

This is Book 1 of the *"Make Money Online Entrepreneur Series"*: *"Freeing Up Your Time – VA's, Outsourcing & Goal Setting"*.

The entire series consists of more than 20 books, specifically written as an entire online business success training course.

Beginning in August 2013, I released one book about every two weeks, in the proper order to ensure success. If you follow the series from Book 1 to the end, one week per book, you will complete a 12-month training course and master being an online entrepreneur! Of course, you can finish the series faster. Just make sure you fully complete the lessons in each book before moving on to the next. This way your success will be greater!

This series is carefully designed to give you every building block you need to build a successful online business. All of the guesswork is taken away, and by following this series, you will avoid most of the common mistakes made by new and even experienced online entrepreneurs. All is revealed – nothing is left out!

The beauty of this series is that you can pick up any book on whatever topic you need at this moment. Or you can purchase each book as it is released. Or ultimately, you can purchase the entire series in a bundle!

However you choose to use the information offered in this and the other books, you will be moving forward with intention and strategy for success in your business.

If at any time you have questions or desire personal one-on-one coaching for a particular topic, feel free to contact me at kip@kippiperbooks.com.

Here's to your online business success!

ONLINE BUSINESS SUCCESS CORE VALUES

Before we get started, it is important to understand, to be a successful online business entrepreneur, it is necessary that you stay focused on your business and have the core values that ensure that success. Here are the values that I have found to be essential to keeping focused and moving forward. These values will be at the beginning of every book of this *"Make Money Online Entrepreneur Series"*.

Be Passionate About Entrepreneurship

As it says, you need to be passionate about what you do and about being an entrepreneur. Being an entrepreneur will present the greatest challenges and the greatest joy you've ever experienced in the business world.

Commit 100% And GO FOR IT

One of the biggest things about being successful is being okay with putting yourself out there. Even if it's just a part-time business, commit 100% of yourself to the time you invest in your business. Commit to see it through and don't give up too soon. As the saying goes, "Don't give up before the miracle happens." Be patient and be persistent.

Build A Network of Support & influence

You must build a network of support and influence. This means building your Facebook community, building your Twitter community, and building your LinkedIn community. You must contribute to other people and help them be successful. By contributing to others and helping them be successful, you will become successful.

Get Comfortable with Being Uncomfortable

You're going to be doing a lot of things that you may or may not have done in the past. You can only grow when you're uncomfortable. When you're feeling comfortable and used to doing the things that you normally do, it's really difficult to grow, so you need to be comfortable with being uncomfortable see you can stretch and grow.

Consistent Growth & Improvement

It is important that you commit to consistent growth and improvement. We all need improvement especially if we are to grow and become successful, because staying up to date with the current tools and resources is essential. What helps you with consistent growth and continuing to improve is tracking your progress on irregular basis.

You also need to be okay with evaluating yourself and looking back at what you did and what you didn't do – without judgment. Simply observe and then recommit to the next step of growth and improvement.

80/20 Rule & Speed of Implementation

I'm sure you would've heard of the 80/20 rule (also known as Pareto's Rule) that 20% of what you do provides 80% of your success. So you need to understand that not everything you do is going to be perfect. Learn from it and move on. The quicker you get things done with the knowledge that you have, the more you'll be able to grow.

Flexible Persistence

Be persistent with everything that you do, and stay consistent with everything you do. The ones who experience the most success are the ones who are persistent in accomplishing their goals and are the most consistent in what they do. To be consistent, you must commit to regularly completing the tasks that ensure your success, whether those tasks occur daily, weekly, monthly, etc.

Surround Yourself With "A" Players

In business you deserve to surround yourself with the best and those who share your entrepreneurial spirit. You become like those you spend your time with. So choose carefully who you hang around with, so you are with those who think like you and make you stretch and reach higher.

The same goes for your employees. If you're going to outsource, you must select the best people who are competent and people you will enjoy working with. Avoid people who have negative attitudes. Surround yourself with those who embrace the concepts of small business success, entrepreneurship, and financial wealth.

Sell With Conviction

Be passionate about your product or service. Make sure you understand every aspect of it so that you can easily describe its features and benefits to your potential customers. If you have hesitations or doubts about your product, improve it so you don't have doubts.

Celebrate All Wins

Celebrate all victories! When you get that first sale, celebrate that first sale. Celebrate each new client. Celebrate each year of business success. Make sure you celebrate all wins. This is really important to maintain passion, momentum and to ensure success.

FREEING UP YOUR TIME & GROWING YOUR COMPANY

In this book, we're going to be talking about freeing up your time and growing your company or your business. This book is all about the concept of outsourcing and leveraging your time.

Most people have heard about outsourcing – taking some of your tasks and not doing them yourself. As an entrepreneur, business owner, or Internet marketer, you need to have the understanding that you can't do everything. You need to be able to leverage other people's time and skill sets in order to grow your business and in order to live the lifestyle and achieve the income you want.

So here's the question:

Why outsource?

You're going to want to outsource tasks that you're not good at – because you can't be good at everything! You may also want to outsource task that you are good at because you can have someone who can do them at least 70 or 80% as well as you can and it will give you time to focus on things that will make you money, otherwise known as "revenue generating activities".

Outsourcing also allows you to grow your company without a lot of capital. With outsourcing, you don't need an office building, you don't need employees and the accompanying benefits, employment taxes, etc.

When you outsource, you have the ability to leverage top-quality talent from anywhere in the world at very low cost. It allows you to do tasks with little or no risk with very minimal capital to get started.

What is the definition of outsourcing?

It does not necessarily mean hiring people offshore at $3 an hour. You can, but sometimes there is the misconception that this is all outsourcing is – the hiring of offshore talent in India, the Philippines, etc., at very low rate. This is not always the case. It can be someone in your own town or anywhere in the United States!

Outsourcing is the ability to give a task to someone outside of your office or home and have it completed.

It can be as simple as a one-off task or item that needs to be completed, or it can be more complex, such as a large, ongoing project.

These are not W-2 employees, meaning that you're not responsible for payroll, payroll taxes, benefits, and all of the other elements that go into having employees. These people are hired on a contract basis as independent contractors. They can be hired hourly or project-based.

It's very important that you understand the distinction that, when we are talking about outsourcing, it does not always mean someone offshore.

When we talk about freeing up your time, we're talking about outsourcing the things you hate doing. One of the benefits of being an entrepreneur is that you can outsource the things that you don't enjoy. If you end up spending time doing a lot of things that you hate and dislike, you may not have the same motivation and passion for your business – and it's very important that you stay motivated and engaged.

Certainly you cannot outsource everything! One of the core rules about outsourcing is having the understanding of the task or project first and then being able to convey it to someone else. It allows you to work at the tasks that you're good at and enjoy.

One of the first steps to outsourcing is evaluating yourself and your expertise. So look deep inside of yourself.

What are your best attributes?
Are you more of a marketing brain?
Are you more of a technical bring?
What do you struggle with?
What do you not enjoy doing?
What type of person would complement your personality?

It is important that you have the understanding that, even though you enjoyed doing something, you can still outsource it because it's not worth your time to do it. It could be a mind-numbing task that someone else could do at a very low rate.

So this was a brief introduction to outsourcing. In this book we will get into a lot more detail about each of these elements of outsourcing.

BENEFITS OF OUTSOURCING

Is chapter, let's explore some of the benefits of outsourcing and why it can be so powerful for both the individual, self-employed sole proprietor or a company with two or three employees.

In the past, you would have had to hire people around your local office. If you needed to hire somebody or find talent, you would typically have to find someone locally, usually by placing an ad in the local newspaper.

But now when you outsource, you have the ability to hire the best! Essentially you have a worldwide talent pool that you can apply tasks to very specific skill sets. In other words, you're not trying to put the proverbial square peg into a round hole. You have the ability to hire for specific tasks those people with the specific skill sets.

Another big benefit is the ability to reduce costs. When you outsource and have either a 1099 contractor or someone who is not a W-2 employee, you don't have to pay employment tax for employees. You have no need for a huge office. You don't have to deal with health insurance for employees or any other benefits. It's a very good option if you have limited start-up capital. It allows you to reduce your costs yet still get high-quality talent to get tasks completed.

Outsourcing is a great for increased contractor retention. You can keep people working for you longer because there is increased flexibility. The people you bring on for your team are typically much happier because they can work remotely. As a consultant/contractor, they get to work on one-off tasks or specific projects, depending on what you need.

Many times when you have employees working together in an office, they can get on each other's nerves. When you outsource, there's not wasted energy and keeping people happy as in an office dynamic.

Another benefit is speed of implementation. Often times what separates the best entrepreneurs and business owners from the others is this one element – speed of implementation – the speed at which they can take an idea/concept/training and get it done. When you use outsource a talent to people who have specific knowledge or skill sets and understand how to do certain things, you don't have to spend time training or get people up to speed. The contractors already have the skill sets and they work on similar tasks and projects on a full-time basis. As a result, you can get things done much then you would otherwise. In my opinion, a benefit of speed of implementation is one of the best things about outsourcing.

There is low risk in outsourcing. You're not committed to 40 hours a week when you outsource, which goes back to reducing costs.

Times there are benefits to having employees in-house. But typically for entrepreneurs and small-business owners, and the small tasks and elements that need to be completed, outsourcing makes the best use of your time and capital.

WHAT TYPES OF TASKS CAN BE OUTSOURCED?

When we talk about freeing up your time and leveraging your time as a business owner and entrepreneur, we need to talk about what types of tasks can be outsourced. In reality, it boils down to any task that can be documented or anything that you don't want to do or don't have the skill set to do.

When I say "anything that can be documented", one of the biggest things you need to do when you outsource different components of your business is you need to be able to document, measure and set expectations for completion and reporting for the people who are doing these tasks for you.

One place many people make mistakes, when they outsource projects or even have employees do projects, is they don't set clear expectations of the results they expect to get back from this relationship – and this is very important.

In this chapter, we're going to segment the types of tasks into two different categories:

- One-off tasks
- Ongoing tasks

A one-off task is a task that is done once and the relationship is basically over. You could also have someone do multiple one-off tasks. A one-off task is not a repeatable process. Possible one-off tasks could be:

- Modification of a website
- Building an element for website
- Writing email copy
- Designing a logo or graphic element

An ongoing task involved an ongoing relationship. It may be a task that is done every week, every month or even every day that the contractor is reporting to you on what they are doing.

As an example, the contractor maybe growing your social media account. You would want someone who can do this every week and report to you on a weekly basis of everything that they have done and the results. You would not have someone just go in, start growing your social media discount and have it be a one-off task for a week. That is not a good situation for that kind of project.

When you are thinking about tasks that can be outsourced, you need to separate your tasks based on whether they are a one-off task or an ongoing task or project.

SOCIAL MEDIA TASKS

In this chapter we are going to be talking about social media tasks that we can outsource. It is important to understand that social media is a great tool that you can leverage as an Internet entrepreneur, and it is one of the easiest ways to build a list and build a following. And the tasks involved in building a list and a following are perfect for outsourcing.

I don't recommend the social media activities that involve interaction as appropriate for outsourcing. Most of the social media tasks that are appropriate for outsourcing revolve around building and growing your presence – not the daily or weekly interaction with your fans and followers.

Let's talk about what different tasks can be outsourced.

Competitive and keyword research

It's important to stay aware about what your competitors are doing in social media. You can outsource the process of that initial competitor analysis across the different social media networks. You can identify the top players in your niche and what they are doing in social media.

Growing Your Contacts – Adding Facebook Friends/Likes and Twitter Followers

You can outsource the growing of your different social media lists, whether it's adding friends to Facebook, adding Twitter followers, adding "likes" to your Facebook page, and adding connections on LinkedIn. General growth strategies and strategically adding people your profiles and pages are perfect for outsourcing.

Join Online Groups and Forums

Another great strategy is to have an outsourced virtual assistant (VA) join online groups and forums for you. When you join groups and forums on Facebook, LinkedIn, Yahoo and Google relevant to your particular niche, you want to have your VA slowly start adding people from within these different groups to your social media profiles.

Status Updates

You must be very careful in how you have your VA post status updates on your behalf to your different social media accounts. You don't want your VA or an outsourced contractor to do all the interaction across your different social media accounts. Why? Because there will be times when a status update posted by a VA will not project your image and personality and your message will not be effectively conveyed.

You don't want the VA to communicate with your friends and followers because you're going to lose that personal connection and your status updates will not come across as genuine and real.

A VA can do general status updates, such as motivational quotes, news links relating to your niche, links to general articles relating to your niche, links to your own blog posts, etc.

You have to be careful about what a VA can do and can share.

When you determine what a VA or an outsourced contractor can do in your social media accounts, the tasks should be centered around growth strategies, growing your presence, or just general communication. Only you should conduct any direct communication with people, such as responses to your posts, etc.

NON-TECHNICAL TASKS

In this chapter we're going to talk about non-technical tasks that you can outsource.

Blogging

The first task that you can outsource is writing your blogs. Having a writer writing keyword-rich blogs can create a consistent pattern of getting quality content to your website. The more quality content you add to your website will build value with your current customers, potential customers and prospects.

A lot of us have the ability to write blogs. However, what you will find when you start to outsource the writing of your blogs, there are a lot of people who can write good, quality content at a very low cost. The cost can be as low as $5-$10 per article – which at this price is not really worth your time to do.

If you are a fantastic writer and can write very quickly, maybe outsourcing this task is not for you. But blogging and writing is certainly a task that I recommend that you outsource. It is a great non-technical task that can be completed by a lot of different people.

Product Creation

Another task that you can outsource is product creation.

This is actually pretty cool! When we talk about creating your first product, you might be the expert and have all of the information, but you may not be the best person to, for instance, record any related videos.

What if you're not the expert? You can find someone who is the expert and have them create that product for you.

Other tasks related to product creation that can be outsourced would be the writing of the product manuals, or creating the PDFs that go along with the product.

When you're considering creating a product, keep in mind that the tasks around some of the elements of the product creation can be outsourced.

Some of the related elements that can be outsourced are sales pages and marketing messages. There is a huge resource of talented marketing professionals and skilled sales writers who can write sales copy for you. With professionally written sales copy, this will definitely increase your conversions.

General Administrative

General administrative tasks are wonderful for outsourcing.

For instance, you could have an email account with general information that a VA could go through and forward the important items to you.

Other general administrative tasks would be growing your social media accounts, posting status updates to your social media accounts, managing your calendar. These are just a few of examples of tasks the remote administrative person could do for you – tasks that bog you down and suck a lot of your time.

Accounting

Accounting and bookkeeping are great tasks to outsource. Find someone to manage your affiliate payments or deposit your checks.

Something that a lot of people don't understand is that non-technical tasks of any sort – whether they relate to your product or your business specifically or whether they are what could be called support services – can be outsourced.

TECHNICAL TASKS

Now let's talk about the technical tasks that can be outsourced.

Graphic Design

An important note before we begin: Some people have the technical skills to do some the things that are covered in this chapter and others don't. For the ones that don't have the skills, it certainly makes sense to outsource these tasks.

However, for this chapter I'm going to talk to those of you who do have these technical skills or perhaps are going to develop the skills as you progress with your Internet business. Even if you have some of the skills, sometimes it makes sense to outsource these tasks because, frankly, your time is worth more than what it costs you to hire someone to complete these tasks at a very low rate.

Some examples are:

- Postcards
- Business cards
- Flyers
- General graphic design elements
- Website graphics
- Logos
- Product logos
- Product layouts, etc.

Even if you have the skills, these tasks can be outsourced very cheaply without a whole lot of management and completed very quickly and easily.

Software and Website Programmers

Very common tasks that are outsourced are software and website programming, building out of specific websites, adding plug-ins to a WordPress blog – anything of technical nature that involves improving your website.

Whether you have great technical skills, have some technical skills, or are totally non-technical, there are technical tasks which are great for outsourcing.

Some of the best Internet marketers and online entrepreneurs have zero technical expertise. What they are good at is understanding what tasks have to be done for their website and then outsourcing to someone who can complete the tasks very easily and very cheaply.

And the reverse is true. There are Internet marketers and online entrepreneurs who have all of the skills handle all of the website development, all of the webpage design, and can build any kind of webpage or sales funnel that they need.

However, when they do all of it themselves, they spent entirely too much time trying to perfect it, build it out, and doing all the technical tasks, and as a result, are sacrificing big dollars because they are bogging themselves down and spending time on tasks that they could very easily outsource.

It's important that you understand what your strengths are, can you do the necessary tasks effectively, should you outsource the tasks. And if you have technical skills, it's important you understand that sometimes it may be more cost effective to outsource these tasks instead of doing them yourself.

BUILDING WEB PRESENCE

Building your web presence is great to outsource. There are a lot of different ways this can be done.

Articles Online

Outsourcing the writing and syndicating of articles online is very effective to building your online presence and getting your name, your company, or your product out there.

There are several different ways to outsource and have someone write quality article content related to your niche. The best thing you can do, however, is to give them a lot of direction. For instance, you could buy them a book for a couple of books that are directly related to your niche or your product. Then have them rewrite something.

The easiest way to get unique, high-quality content that is relevant to your niche through outsourcing is to have the person rewrite content that you already like.

Typically, articles are 300 to 700 words in length. It is important that every article have links and other information that will tie in to your product or your niche.

Videos Online

You can have your VA or contractor submit videos to YouTube or create videos that are relevant to your keyword and include links to your website, etc. There are a lot different elements that can be outsourced when it comes to the writing, creation, editing, etc., of web videos and promoting videos online.

Editing and rendering video – for a more professional presentation – is a specialized technical skill that is always best to be outsourced. There are tons of people on the web that will edit and render your videos quickly, easily and cheaply.

Building Website Content

Hire a writer to write keyword-rich blogs and getting new content on your site. Make sure you hire someone who understands the power of keywords and understands the type of content you want.

Links Back to Your Site

Link building – getting links back to your site and links back to your product – is a great strategy for SEO and building your online presence. One of the rankings that Google recognizes when ranking for SEO is the inbound links back to your site. So have a VA or outsource contractor research the web for blogs, forums, social media sites, etc., and build links back to your website.

Link building and other web presence building strategies do not happen overnight. So you will find when you employ a VA to slowly and consistently build your online presence, over time you will definitely build a much bigger and stronger presence.

Social Media Growth

Social media growth and general social media forums and group posts are some things that a VA can accomplish. This will build your presence and build you as an expert in your niche – very quickly and easily.

COSTS OF OUTSOURCING

Let's ask the question that is on everyone's mind:

How much does outsourcing cost?

Frankly, it depends on a lot of different things:

- The type of task or project
- The level of skill you want to employ to complete the task or project
- How many people can perform this task or project
    - o The more general the skill and the more people that can do it, the cheaper the cost)
- Domestic or offshore
    - o When you hire within the US, the UK, and Australia, the cost is typically more expensive than if you hire offshore.
    - o The communication and feedback may be easier when you hire within the US, versus hiring offshore where you have potential language and cultural differences.
    - o You may get better quality locally than when you hire offshore.

When outsourcing, you need to make sure when you post a job that you were very detailed in the description and the skills required. This way a lot of people can bid on the project. Then you could make the most educated decision in hiring the best person for the project.

When it comes to cost, the cheapest is not always the best. However, a lot of times the cheapest will be the best choice for you because of the type of project. Frankly, the cost is going to change from project to project and to where you're outsourcing.

As a general rule, "local" outsourcing means within the United States, the UK and Australia and will be a little more expensive. Outsourcing "offshore" means India, the Philippines, and some Eastern European countries and you will pay a little bit less.

You need to understand that some projects are just fine to outsource offshore. As you become more experienced with outsourcing and more comfortable with outsourcing for different projects, it becomes easier for you to outsource offshore and conquer any language for cultural differences.

Say you're just getting started, and you have a project which will take only half an hour. If your contractor rates are $12 an hour locally versus $6 an hour offshore, then it may make sense to pay a little bit more to have a slightly more qualified person or someone with whom it is easier to communicate, so you're not wasting time with any communication issue.

As you become more experienced with the process of outsourcing, you will have a much is your time outsourcing to anywhere.

Protecting Yourself and Your Money

When outsourcing, you need to make sure you're protecting yourself and protecting your money.

I strongly recommend online work environments that protect you from any sort of scam and possibly putting your money at risk.

Online work environments include sites like:

- Elance.com
- ODesk.com

(Actually there are more sites out there! See "My Outsourcing Experience" below and later chapter "Examples of Online Work Environments".)

The big benefits are not only the fact that we can find people with whom to outsource on these sites, but the sites also protect us, meaning both our interests and the interests of contractor are both protected. I am responsible to pay but I'm only responsible to pay for work that is completed.

In outsourcing, protecting yourself and protecting your money is very important. That's why I strongly recommend working within an online work environment when outsourcing.

My Outsourcing Experience

Since February 2012, I have had a full-time virtual assistant from the Philippines. She is wonderful! Her cost to me is just $85 per week. This is a little more than $15 per day – triple the average daily income in the Philippines. Plus I often give her bonuses when she meets a tight deadline. Needless to say, this is value for both of us!

I have also hired several "one-off task" contractors through elance.com and odesk.com, with much success. Only once I have I had to cancel a job because of non-performance of the contractor, and odesk.com was wonderful in helping resolve the issue.

I strongly encourage you to consider hiring outside of the US. Many cultures have extremely talented people and their work ethic is unsurpassed. I learned how to hire offshore from:

James Wedmore's online training course "6 Figure Outsourcing Secrets"
http://kippiperbooks.com/6FOS

It is well worth the modest investment to learn how to correctly post an ad, effectively interview to find the best candidate, and how to manage your offshore employee to ensure loyalty and great results.

COMMUNICATION

One a very important component of outsourcing is communication.

A great benefit of outsourcing is that you don't have someone sitting next to you all day, every day in your office. However, with outsourcing, communication is not only still key, but probably even more important.

When you outsource and are in a remote environment, you need to make sure there is a high level of connection and communication on a consistent basis. This communication does not have to be anything big or involved, just a set method of communication that both you and the contractor understand.

Always Build TRUST

You want to develop a feeling of comfort and build trust your VA's and contractors. Your VA's and contractors want to know they are appreciated and feel part of the team. If you have ongoing work, you want to make them aware of it and keep reminding them of it. You don't want to be overbearing, but keep on top of the fact that it is a relationship of two-way communication. If it is a good outsourcing contractor or VA, you want to make sure that you manage that relationship effectively.

On the other hand, if you are running out of work or a project is coming to a close, the honest with your contractor or VA. Let them know when they can expect the project to be over. That way they can prepare their calendar. You don't want to put them in a bad situation if they've committed to certain number of hours a week to you and they're expecting this to be ongoing. If you cut the work off without proper notice, you can burn a bridge and they're not going to want to reciprocate that kind of courtesy back to you if you ever want to work with them again in the future.

When I talk about consistently reaching out to them, even if they're not currently working for you and they've done good work in the past, send them an email every couple of weeks or once a month. Something simple like, "Good day! I hope everything is going well with you." And perhaps just a little update of what's going on with you and your company. Just reach out, build and maintain that connection and let them know you're still around. Then when you do contact them a few months down the road, they will remember who you are. It's really important.

Review Process

You need to make sure you have a good review process when you are working with your VA or contractor. As they complete tasks, you need to make sure that there are goals in place.

You don't want to allow large projects to go forward without progress being checked along the way. So you want to take bigger projects and break them into smaller segments, smaller goals. Literally, this can be as small as what they are accomplishing on a daily or weekly basis.

Here's a great tip: You want to have the funds that you are releasing for payment of the project to be released in small amounts, as these goals are being completed. In other words, you are tying the goals to the money. This gives the VA or contractor incentive to complete the goals. It also prevents you as the employer from paying a lot of money without a commensurate amount of work being completed.

This method of releasing funds as goals enhances the building of trust. It also allows for making the project move along in a fashion that works well for you and works well for your contractor. This is a mutual relationship where both parties are benefiting and communicating.

Encourage Workers to Visit the Office or Meet in Person

If you have the ability and have workers who are close by, encourage them to visit your office or meet you in person. If your virtual assistants are local or if you are traveling to where they are located, stop in or set up a meeting, such as for coffee. Obviously if they're located offshore, it's is an unlikely scenario. But if it's someone in your general area, it goes a long way. It shows them you're serious about the relationship and it will allow for a mutually beneficial relationship to go forward.

Rewarding, Motivating, Coaching

If you have a VA or contractor that you enjoy working with and they hit their goals, sometimes it makes sense to give them a little extra bonus and reward them financially. Maybe with a meal, gift card, or even a little extra money. Motivate them in the weekly calls, encourage them to present their ideas, make them feel important.

Another idea is, if you have an online course or book that you use and is important for your business, give them access to it or purchase the course or book for them. Give them information that will help them improve or leverage existing information you have that can improve the overall result you get from them.

In summary, when we talk about communicating with your VA's or contractors, the important points are:

- There is consistent communication.
- There are clearly defined goals and a review process.
- There is an element of communication outside the work environment where you try to communicate with them, from time to time, on a more personal level – particularly if you're not currently working with them but have projects for them down the road.
- There is a system in place to reward, motivate, and coach them so they can be better at what they do for you.

Communication is key so you can make sure the relationship is mutually beneficial in both the short and long term.

TIPS FOR A SUCCESSFUL RELATIONSHIP

In this chapter we're going to talk about tips for successful relationship with your outsourced VA or contractor.

Try a Trial Run

The first tip is to have a trial run. Even if you have a big, ongoing task or project for which you need to hire someone to implement and complete, one of the best things you can do is hire someone for one or two small tasks first. Even if you're fully confident that this person will be great, hiring them for just one or two small tasks will allow you to see exactly how they work, how they report, and making sure you really are comfortable with them before you give them a really big, important project.

If you don't give them a trial run first, you take the risk of handing off a big project to them, realizing they are not a good fit, and then having to start all over again.

When you have a trial run first, this is a great method to start and build a great relationship for now and in the future.

Simple Consistent Tasks

When you can outsource simple consistent tasks, it will always be a better situation than outsourcing big complex projects.

If you do have a big complex project to outsource, one of the ways to ensure a greater chance of success is to break up that project into simple tasks and then outsource those simple tasks. The smaller, simple tasks allow for easier communication and realistic expectations.

Another example is, if you want to hire one person for one task, have that one person do that one task every week. Don't necessarily try to keep one person busy for 40 hours a week. It's the old concept of putting all of your eggs in one basket. What happens if they stop like working for you, or conversely, you're not happy with their results? Sometimes it's more beneficial to have a few different outsourced VA's doing a few different tasks rather than one person doing a lot of different things for you.

BENEFITS OF ONLINE WORK ENVIRONMENTS

In this chapter we're going to discuss the benefits of online work environments to you as a business owner or entrepreneur.

Ability to Review Online Portfolios and Resumes

With an online work environment, you have the ability to review online portfolios and resumes.

If you post a job and people apply, you can review the portfolios of the applicants and examples of work they have done in the past. You can also look at their resume, their experience, their skill sets, etc. You can learn a lot about people prior to them even knowing that you're interested in possibly hiring them. This puts you in the best possible position and gives you an advantage before you get into the hiring process.

Ability to Review Testimonials

You also have the ability to review testimonials – both the positive and the negative feedback. By reading the testimonials, you can learn what a previous employer has to say about the applicant.

It's important to read at least most if not all of the testimonials.

- Look for the size and cost of the projects identified in the testimonials.
- Were the projects short-term or long-term.
- Were the projects similar to the project you are posting.

If the project you're wanting to outsource is a longer term project with consistent reporting, and it looks like the only projects the applicant has worked on were weekly or one-off projects, this applicant probably is not

33

the right fit for your project.

Conversely, if you have a one-off project and the applicant is used to completing long-term projects, this applicant may also not be a good fit.

You want to try to find out as much information as possible, and read the testimonials and feedback – both positive and negative – about the applicants you are considering.

Ability to Review Previous Job Rankings

Next you have the ability to review previous job rankings.

When employers post jobs and VA's are hired, the VA's employment history is listed in the online at work environment. This allows you to see each VA's or contractor's past experience. Each job is listed, along with:

- Description of the job
- Type of job
- Date of the job
- Payment amount
- Hourly rate
- Fixed payment or by the hour
- Feedback from the employer
- If there are current ongoing jobs
- Etc.

Seeing if the applicant has current ongoing jobs is important to know. If the applicant you are considering has 8 or 10 current ongoing projects just within that one work environment, they probably are not the right fit at this time because they may not have the time to probably devote to your project. This is very important to take into account when you're considering online contractors.

Ability to Track Ongoing Progress

One of the best benefits I think of hiring someone through Elance.com or ODesk.com is your ability to track your VA's or contractor's ongoing progress.

As an example, ODesk.com takes a screenshot of the VA's computer every 15 minutes when they are working on your project. This is because the VA logs into the ODesk.com system when they begin working on your project, and every 15 minutes or so the system will automatically take a screenshot of the VA's computer screen to see what is being worked on.

So let's say the VA says they logged five hours working on your project.

You will have 15 to 20 different screenshots that were taken over that period of time so you can see exactly what they were doing when and their progress.

Bottom line, you know they were actually working on your task or project and not overbilling you. This goes back to protecting your money and receiving the most value from the money you are paying to hire for these particular tasks or projects.

Manage Payments and Escrow Protection

Another benefit to the online work environments is being able to manage payments and escrow protection of your different projects. The online work environments protect you from scams and put your money into escrow. This is a benefit in two ways:

- It protects the contractor because you have deposited the money into the escrow account, so they know you have the ability to pay them which provides a level of comfort and trust.
  - If the work is done in accordance to the agreement, the contractor know you will pay them because the money is sitting in the third-party escrow account provided by the online work environment.
  - When the project is completed and the goal is reached, you will sign off to release the funds to the contractor.
  - This provides incentive to the contractor to get the work done.
- It protects you as an employer from someone taking your money and not delivering the work.

Managing payments through escrow really helps these online work environments create trust for both the employer and the contractor.

How Many Hours Have They Billed

An online work environment allows you to track how many hours has your VA or contractor billed. This is beneficial in helping you understand how the VA or contractor works and are they more likely to deliver a product or service better if it's a big project or a small task. You can clearly see the past history of all the different applicants.

Based on my experience, the more you hire applicants for tasks and projects they are used to – maybe hourly, or by total time over the course of a month, or project by project – the more you can work with what they are used to, the more likelihood of success.

Test Results

A great benefit of online working environments is your ability to see an applicant's test results. Within most online working environments, the applicant has the opportunity to take tests for a variety of skills, such as typing speed, data entry, different software platforms (Joomla, PHP, et. al.), Microsoft products, Adobe products, WordPress, etc. Each applicant is then ranked based on their results against the other people who have taken the tests within that specific online working environment.

In reviewing the ranking of each applicant, you have to use your judgment as to how their ranking compares to your project requirements. For instance, if an applicant ranks at the 75% proficiency level for Microsoft Word, this could mean that they can handle basic Microsoft Word functions but not the more sophisticated features. If all you need are the basic functions, then this person could work well for you and save you money because they cannot charge as high a rate as someone who has a 90% or 95% proficiency level.

With the test results, you have a deeper picture into the skill sets of the different applicants you were considering prior to hiring them.

Filter Who Sees Your Project

One of the last benefits of online work environments allows you to filter who sees your project.

In other words, you do not necessarily have to post your project for what is called an "open" bid. Instead, you can create a task and search for applicants that you feel meet your project description.

Why is this a benefit? It eliminates a potentially overwhelming number of people applying for your project, and allows you to prescreen potential applicants.

You can filter by a number of variables, such as:

- Geographic region or country
- Price range
- Skill sets
- Etc.

This helps you identify the right potential applicants and not waste your time evaluating applicants who in no way would be a good fit. The more you can filter who sees your project, the better it will be for you in being efficient throughout the hiring process.

EXAMPLES OF ONLINE WORK ENVIRONMENTS

We have discussed the benefits of outsourcing, types of tasks to be outsourced, and other aspects of outsourcing. Now here are some examples of places where you can find good VA's and contractors. Many of online work environments also give you the previously discussed benefits, such as, the ability to track work progress, review profiles, review test results, see previous projects and previous employer feedback.

www.Elance.com
Elance is one of the biggest and baddest freelance websites and has contractors who are looking to do projects of all sizes and types – everything from social media to SEO to basic design to writing services – basically everything under the sun.

www.oDesk.com
ODesk has a lot of the same features.

www.Rent-ACoder.com
Rent-aCoder is more of a technical online work environment for things such as website design, website functionality, programming, etc.

www.freelance.com

www.guru.com

So here are five good online work environment websites. There are many other sites on the Internet. I have listed these because my clients and myself have had good experiences with them.

HIRING PROCESS

So now you're ready to hire a VA, or perhaps you've already done so in the past. In this chapter were going to discuss all about the specific things you want to do make sure your hiring process delivers to you a VA or contractor whom you can rely on and is going to deliver to you the result you want to achieve. In the end, that is the most important thing.

Phone Interview (NOT Email!)

The first thing you want to do is to make sure you have a phone interview – *not* just email. This is probably one of the biggest things most people overlook. They will communicate just by email and not have a phone interview.

When I say "phone interview", this can also be via Skype or Google Talk. The point is you are definitely going to want to have a voice communication with your potential contractor. This is critical.

In the phone interview you want to ask the questions that relate to your project. At the end of the interview, you want to ask yourself a few questions:

- Does the person understand your business, what you do, what you want to achieve?
    - o Obviously you need to convey that to them, and it's also important that they understand what you're looking to achieve.
- Was the person easy to talk to?
    - o Sometimes you will hire VA's from other countries and there will be an accent or communication barrier. From my experience, there is a wide varying degree of this

communication issue when we are talking about dealing with VA's from other countries. There will be different requirements for different people, meaning some people can communicate with people who don't speak perfect English and others simply can't. So if you are person who needs better verbal communication and for your contractor to have a better understanding of the English language, make sure you acknowledge that about yourself. Also make sure you can communicate effectively with your contractor.

- Were there any communication problems?
  - o You want to make sure you can connect with them and communicate effectively with the person you may potentially hire.

Interview Many VA's

In the next part of the hiring process you want to interview many VA's and contractors.

You're not going to talk to just one applicant and then hire them. You want to talk to at least a few different people. This gives you a baseline you can reference against when considering each applicant.

If you interview only one person for particular job, how will you compare them with anyone else? You might assume this person is the best out there or sufficient. However, if you spend the time – an extra 15 minutes or so – to have another phone interview with another potential candidate, you may find someone better for that project.

It's very important that you interview more than one person.

Also, it's vital that you interview the person who will actually be doing the work. An applicant may be a VA who has other VA's that work for them. You want to be sure to ask if this is the case. Is the person you are interviewing the one who will actually perform the work or are they a middleman?

If they are a middleman, you don't necessarily have to eliminate them. You just want to make sure you understand if the person you're interviewing will be doing the work or if they are a middleman. Plus you need to understand who will be communicating with you, who will be completing the work, etc.

Do They Have Experience Working Remotely?

This is really important – does the applicant have experience working remotely?

Sometimes you might be hiring someone through Elance.com or ODesk.com that might be new to working remotely. You need to directly ask them if they have experience working remotely.

Some of the applicants maybe new to freelance work or maybe they're looking to supplement their income in addition to their full-time job. You need to hire someone who has experience in working remotely.

One way to test this throughout the interview process is, if they have a Skype name? Most people will have Skype If you don't have Skype, you should get it – it's a free tool that you can leverage.

Next, check to see how often do they log into Skype. Most contractors are going to be familiar with Skype. In my experience, you will find that the contractors that are the easiest to get in touch with are the ones on Skype. If you've never used Skype before, there is a simple little indicator – a green checkmark – that shows when people are online. You can easily see if they are online and available. In the interview and hiring process, just check to see if they are online on Skype. If they are, typically they're going to be more accessible.

Response Time During Interview Process

Along these lines, you're going to want to follow and track the response time during the interview and hiring process for VA's and contractors.

If you're hiring a VA for potential job, and they don't have a quick, timely response time or they're not getting back to you in a timeframe that works for you, do you honestly think that once they get the job that their response time is going to all of a sudden get better?

Response times are probably going to be best when they are applying to or trying to get jobs. Their response time is a true indicator of how that relationship is going to work.

So pay attention to how quickly they are responding to your emails. Remember, they might be in a different time zone. So if you haven't laid out expectations for a response time, just make sure you understand where they are located geographically. So if you email them at two in the morning and they haven't got back with you within six or seven hours, you may have to consider that they are in a different times.

Does it take them days to respond? Do they log into Skype only once every three days? You should definitely get an idea during the interview process of what their response time is going to be. Honestly, if you don't pay attention to that and you hire a VA or contractor that didn't have great response time during the hiring process, I can assure you that it's only going to get worse once you actually hire them.

So make sure you are monitoring response times during the interview process.

WEEKLY AND DAILY BUSINESS GOALS

One of the most important elements of being a successful entrepreneur is being able to efficiently and effectively manage your time. The best way to do this is to set consistent goals and also by time blocking your days and your weeks to make sure you're focusing on getting things done. The concepts of goal setting and time blocking will allow you to get more things done is shorter amounts of time. As an entrepreneur, the more we can get done and the more efficiently we can operate, the more profitable any business venture will be.

You want to set goals that you are able to accomplish but you don't want to set goals that are too easy or don't push you at all. If you're able to work efficiently and effectively, you should be able to complete 80% of your daily and weekly goals. This means there will be a few goals on your weekly and daily goal sheet that will be a little bit difficult for you to achieve, and that's okay.

At the same time you want to be sure not to set too lofty a goal or too lofty expectations which result in you meeting only 15 or 20% of your weekly or daily goals. That would be very discouraging!

So the magic number is 80%!

For a sample weekly goal sheet, at the end of this book is the download link for the bonus "Weekly Business Goals".

BONUS MATERIALS

Below are links to this book's bonus materials. I have developed these tools from my own experience as well as compiled from tools I have used from various training courses I have taken.

The mind maps are built in XMind software. You can download a free version of XMind from **http://xmind.net**.

All items are available as PDFs.

Strategic Plan – VA's, Outsourcing & Goal Setting Mind Map
http://www.kippiperbooks.com/make-money-online/book01/Strategic_Plan_VAs_Outsourcing_Goal_Setting.xmind

Strategic Plan – VA's, Outsourcing & Goal Setting PDF
http://www.kippiperbooks.com/make-money-online/book01/Strategic_Plan_VAs_Outsourcing_Goal_Setting.pdf

This strategic plan will help guide you through the processes discussed in this book. This is only a plan! Feel free to modify to meet your needs.

What to Outsource Mind Map
http://www.kippiperbooks.com/make-money-online/book01/What_To_Outsource.xmind

What to Outsource PDF
http://www.kippiperbooks.com/make-money-online/book01/What_To_Outsource.pdf

VA Hiring Process Mind Map
http://www.kippiperbooks.com/make-money-online/book01/VA_Hiring_Process.xmind

VA Hiring Process PDF
http://www.kippiperbooks.com/make-money-online/book01/VA_Hiring_Process.pdf

Weekly Business Goals – Blank Excel Spreadsheet
http://www.kippiperbooks.com/make-money-online/book01/Weekly_Business_Goals_Blank.xlsx

Weekly Business Goals – Blank PDF
http://www.kippiperbooks.com/make-money-online/book01/Weekly_Business_Goals_Blank.pdf

RESOURCES

James Wedmore's online training course
6 Figure Outsourcing Secrets
This course is well worth the modest investment to learn how to correctly post an ad, effectively interview to find the best candidate, and how to manage your offshore employee to ensure loyalty and great results.
Here is the URL to learn more about this course:

http://kippiperbooks.com/6FOS

www.Elance.com
Elance is one of the biggest and baddest freelance websites and has contractors who are looking to do projects of all sizes and types – everything from social media to SEO to basic design to writing services – basically everything under the sun.

www.oDesk.com
ODesk has a lot of the same features.

www.Rent-ACoder.com
Rent-aCoder is more of a technical online work environment for things such as website design, website functionality, programming, etc.

www.freelance.com

www.guru.com

MORE KINDLE BOOKS BY KIP PIPER

Ultimate Affiliate Marketing with Blogging Quick Start Guide
http://www.kippiperbooks.com/UltimateGuide

Make Money Online Entrepreneur Series:

Below are just a few of the books in this series. To browse the entire series, go to:
http://www.kippiperbooks.com/makemoneyonlineseries

Book 1 – Freeing Up Your Time – VA's, Outsourcing & Goal Setting
http://www.kippiperbooks.com/book1
Book 2 – Your Core Business, Niche & Competitors
http://www.kippiperbooks.com/book2
Book 3 – Blogs & Emails: Your Link with Your Customers
http://www.kippiperbooks.com/book3
Book 4 – Affiliate Marketing 101
http://www.kippiperbooks.com/book4
Book 5 - Driving Traffic with Organic SEO
http://www.kippiperbooks.com/book5
Book 6 – Power of Email Marketing
http://www.kippiperbooks.com/book6
Book 7 – Quick Income Formula with Advanced Affiliate Marketing
http://www.kippiperbooks.com/book7
Book 8 – List Building with Facebook
http://www.kippiperbooks.com/book8
Book 9 – List Building with Twitter
http://www.kippiperbooks.com/book9
Book 10 - List Building with LinkedIn
http://www.kippiperbooks.com/book10

ONE LAST THING...

As you can probably tell from my writing, my intention is to inspire and support more people to build a better financial future. It's a tough economy today, and I think personal growth in the field of small business is more important than ever before. Even though I have well over 20 years of experience as a successful small business owner and online entrepreneur, I don't have all the answers. In fact I'm still learning myself, I just have my own opinions, experiences and a passion for being my own boss to guide me through life.

Thank you purchasing my eBook and for taking the time to read it. I hope you enjoyed it and found value within its pages.

If you did I would really appreciate your support by taking the time to write a review for me on Amazon. Reviews really help the authors you enjoy to get noticed in a crowded marketplace, and it would allow me to continue writing the books for this series and other business books.

Please visit the URL below to let me know your thoughts:

http://kippiperbooks.com/book1

All of my books are offered completely FREE on the launch and I want to reward loyal readers by offering my new books to them FREE of charge when they are released.

So please visit my website KipPiperBooks.com and either download your free copy of *"28-Day Small Business Profit Plan: The Quick Start Guide to Business Success"* or just sign up to my newsletter in order to be kept informed when the next release is due. I hate spam, so I promise I won't share your information with anyone – not for love nor money!

Good luck! I wish you every success in your personal and business endeavors.

www.ingramcontent.com/pod-product-compliance
Lightning Source LLC
Chambersburg PA
CBHW071327200326

41520CB00013B/2886